200 Sight Words Activity Workbook

This book belongs to

Hello!
I am Isabela and my passion is introducing kids to the wonderful world of letters and numbers.
I want you to experience how fun writing can be! This is why I have created this 200 Sight Words Workbook.
So, if you liked this book encourage your parents to leave a review.
Your thoughts and opinions are very important to me.
This is how I keep creating workbooks like this!
Also, as a bonus, when your book is completed you can claim a free certificate by following the instructions at the end of the workbook.
Thank you!
Hi!
I am buzzy. I want to be your friend and guide you through the journey of learning.
We'll have so much fun together!

What are Sight Words?

Sight words are the words that appear most frequently in our reading and writing. They are called "sight" words because the goal is for your child to recognize these words instantly, at first sight. A couple of examples of sight words are: "a, me, to, be, with, go, after, every".

By eliminating the need to stop and decode sight words, children are able to focus on words that are less familiar and more difficult. Teaching sight words not only helps students read more fluently, but it also helps them write more efficiently too. You will be happy to know that this 200 Sight Words Workbook features words from the Dolch and Fry high-frequency word lists.

Did you know?

- Sight words appear often in a text.
- They give meaning and direction to language.
- They also provide clues to the context of the text.
- These words comprise 80% of the words you would find in a typical children's book.

Dolch Sight Words List

Edward William Dolch (b. 1889, d. 1961) was a prolific writer of academic texts and articles about reading. He developed the "Dolch Sight Words List" for the purpose of making learning English much more easy and efficient for children. His list consists of 220 words.

The best way to learn?

In the early stages of learning, children often need the help of a parent, teacher, or caregiver in order to gain a clear understanding of language.

The best approach to learn sight words is to:

- Write and spell the word and the sentence.
- Comprehend its use in a simple sentence.
- Emphasize how the word is used in the context of that phrase through a visual representation.

Fry Sight Words List

Dr. Edward Fry (b. 1925, d. 2010) wrote widely on how to teach reading.

He created the "Fry Sight Words List" that includes the most common words used in English. These words must be easily recognized by children in order to achieve reading fluency. Fry's Instant Words is comprised of 1000 words.

Part 1
Let's recap the alphabet!

Trace the uppercase letters and then practice writing them on your own in the remaining space!

A A A A A

B B B B

C C C C

D D D D

E E E E

F F F F

G G G G

H H H H

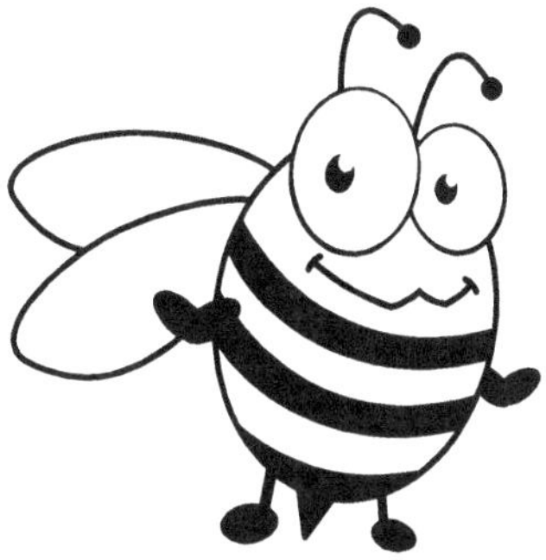

I   I I I   I I I   I I I

J   J J J   J J J   J J J

K   K K K   K K K   K K K

L   L L L   L L L   L L L

M   M M M   M M M   M M M

N   N N N   N N N   N N N

O   O O O   O O O   O O O

P   P P P   P P P   P P P

Q   Q Q Q   Q Q Q   Q Q Q

R	R R R
S	S S S
T	T T T
U	U U U
V	V V V
W	W W W
X	X X X
Y	Y Y Y
Z	Z Z Z

Trace the lowercase letters and then practice writing them on your own in the remaining space!

a a a a

b b b b

c c c c

d d d d

e e e e

f f f f

g g g g

h h h h

Trace the lowercase letters and then practice writing them on your own in the remaining space!

i i i i i

j j j j j

k k k k k

l l l l l

m m m m m

n n n n n

o o o o o

p p p p p

q q q q q

Trace the lowercase letters and then practice writing them on your own in the remaining space!

r r r r

s s s s

t t t t

u u u u

v v v v

w w w w

x x x x

y y y y

z z z z

Part 2
Write 1 & 2 letter words

My sight word: a

Read the following sentence!

I have a book.

Trace and write the sentence!

I have a book.

Color the picture!

My sight word: am

Read the following sentence!

I am a teacher.

Trace and write the sentence!

I am a teacher.

Color the picture!

My sight word:

as

Read the following sentence!

I work as a dog trainer.

Trace and write the sentence!

I work as a dog trainer.

Color the picture!

My sight word: an

Read the following sentence!

Paris is an amazing city.

Trace and write the sentence!

Paris is an amazing city.

Color the picture!

My sight word: at

Read the following sentence!

The girl smiled at me.

Trace and write the sentence!

The girl smiled at me.

Color the picture!

My sight word: **be**

Read the following sentence!

I will be at the cinema.

Trace and write the sentence!

I will be at the cinema.

Color the picture!

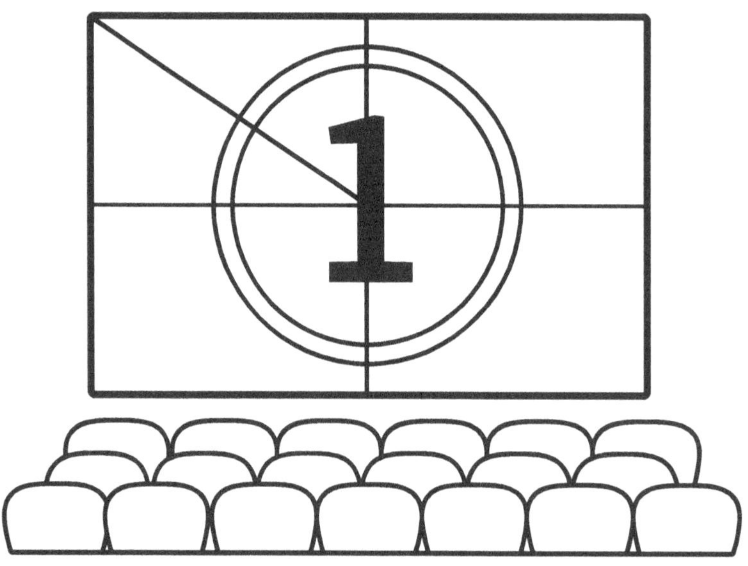

My sight word: by

Read the following sentence!

I must be in bed by 9 o'clock.

Trace and write the sentence!

I must be in bed by 9 o'clock.

Color the picture!

My sight word: **do**

Read the following sentence!

Do you like my puzzle?

Trace and write the sentence!

Do you like my puzzle?

Color the picture!

My sight word:

go

Read the following sentence!

Let's go to the park.

Trace and write the sentence!

Let's go to the park.

Color the picture!

My sight word: he

Read the following sentence!

He runs very fast.

Trace and write the sentence!

He runs very fast.

Color the picture!

My sight word: I

Read the following sentence!

I like to dance.

Trace and write the sentence!

I like to dance

Color the picture!

My sight word: **if**

Read the following sentence!

If it rains we will get wet.

Trace and write the sentence!

If it rains we will get wet.

Color the picture!

My sight word: in

Read the following sentence!

There is a tree in the garden.

Trace and write the sentence!

There is a tree in the garden.

Color the picture!

My sight word: is

Read the following sentence!

What time is it?

Trace and write the sentence!

What time is it?

Color the picture!

My sight word:

Read the following sentence!

It is a snowy day.

Trace and write the sentence!

It is a snowy day.

Color the picture!

My sight word: me

Read the following sentence!

Mom is proud of me.

Trace and write the sentence!

Mom is proud of me.

Color the picture!

My sight word:  my

 **Read the following sentence!**

My family is the best.

 **Trace and write the sentence!**

My family is the best.

 **Color the picture!**

My sight word: no

Read the following sentence!

She has no pets.

Trace and write the sentence!

She has no pets.

Color the picture!

My sight word: of

Read the following sentence!

He is part of the karate team.

Trace and write the sentence!

He is part of the karate team.

Color the picture!

My sight word: 

on

Read the following sentence!

The flowers are on the table.

Trace and write the sentence!

The flowers are on the table.

Color the picture!

My sight word: or

Read the following sentence!

Do you want a dog or a cat?

Trace and write the sentence!

Do you want a dog or a cat?

Color the picture!

My sight word: SO

Read the following sentence!

It is raining, so we play inside.

Trace and write the sentence!

It is raining, so we play inside.

Color the picture!

My sight word: to

Read the following sentence!

I like to paint flowers.

Trace and write the sentence!

I like to paint flowers.

Color the picture!

My sight word:

up

 **Read the following sentence!**

Hurry up! We will be late.

 **Trace and write the sentence!**

Hurry up! We will be late.

 **Color the picture!**

My sight word: **us**

Read the following sentence!

You make us happy.

Trace and write the sentence!

You make us happy.

Color the picture!

My sight word: **we**

Read the following sentence!

We want to see the puppies.

Trace and write the sentence!

We want to see the puppies.

Color the picture!

Part 3
Write 3 letter words

My sight word:

add

Read the following sentence!

Let's add milk to the list.

Trace and write the sentence!

Let's add milk to the list.

Color the picture!

My sight word:

air

Read the following sentence!

We go out for some fresh air.

Trace and write the sentence!

We go out for some fresh air.

Color the picture!

My sight word: all

Read the following sentence!

All of my friends like soccer.

Trace and write the sentence!

All of my friends like soccer.

Color the picture!

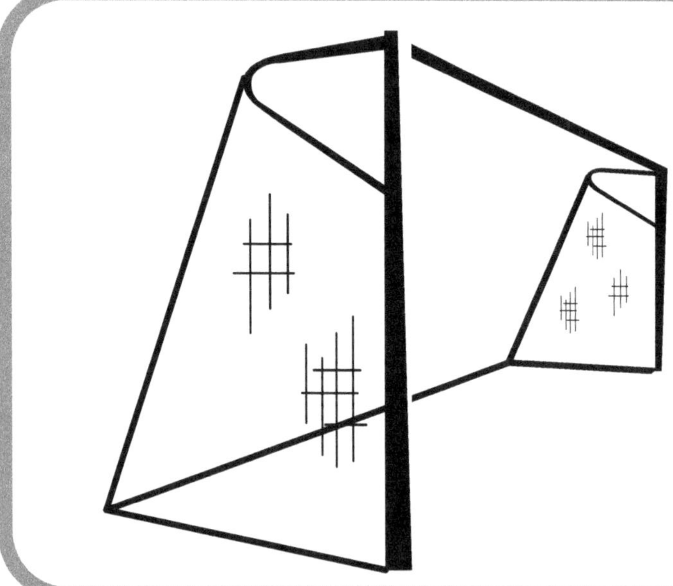

My sight word: **and**

Read the following sentence!

She and I are friends.

Trace and write the sentence!

She and I are friends.

Color the picture!

My sight word: any

Read the following sentence!

I don't have any appels.

Trace and write the sentence!

I don't have any appels

Color the picture!

My sight word: **are**

Read the following sentence!

They are my grandparents.

Trace and write the sentence!

They are my grandparents.

Color the picture!

My sight word: big

Read the following sentence!

We live near a big supermarket.

Trace and write the sentence!

We live near a big supermarket.

Color the picture!

My sight word: **but**

Read the following sentence!

I want to sleep but I am not tired.

Trace and write the sentence!

I want to sleep but I am not tired.

Color the picture!

My sight word: can

Read the following sentence!

Can you help me with my homework.

Trace and write the sentence!

Can you help me with my homework?

Color the picture!

My sight word:

car

Read the following sentence!

My favorite toy is a car.

Trace and write the sentence!

My favorite toy is a car.

Color the picture!

My sight word: cat

Read the following sentence!

The cat is on the chair.
• • • • • •

Trace and write the sentence!

The cat is on the chair.

Color the picture!

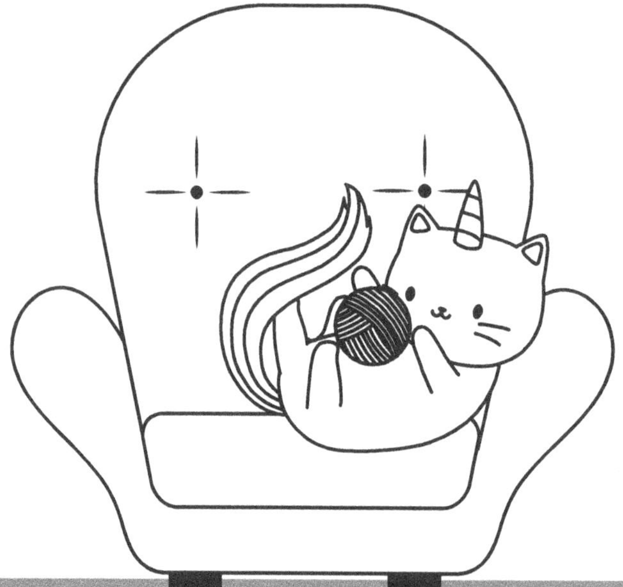

My sight word: day

Read the following sentence!

It is a sunny day.

Trace and write the sentence!

It is a sunny day.

Color the picture!

My sight word: did

Read the following sentence!

Did you feed the dog?

Trace and write the sentence!

Did you feed the dog?

Color the picture!

My sight word: dog

 **Read the following sentence!**

We are getting a dog.

 **Trace and write the sentence!**

We are getting a dog.

 **Color the picture!**

My sight word:

eat

Read the following sentence!

I always eat my vegetables.

Trace and write the sentence!

I always eat my vegetables.

Color the picture!

My sight word:

fly

 **Read the following sentence!**

Let's fly a kite.

 **Trace and write the sentence!**

Let's fly a kite.

 **Color the picture!**

My sight word: for

Read the following sentence!

We will have pancakes for breakfast.

Trace and write the sentence!

We will have pancakes for breakfast.

Color the picture!

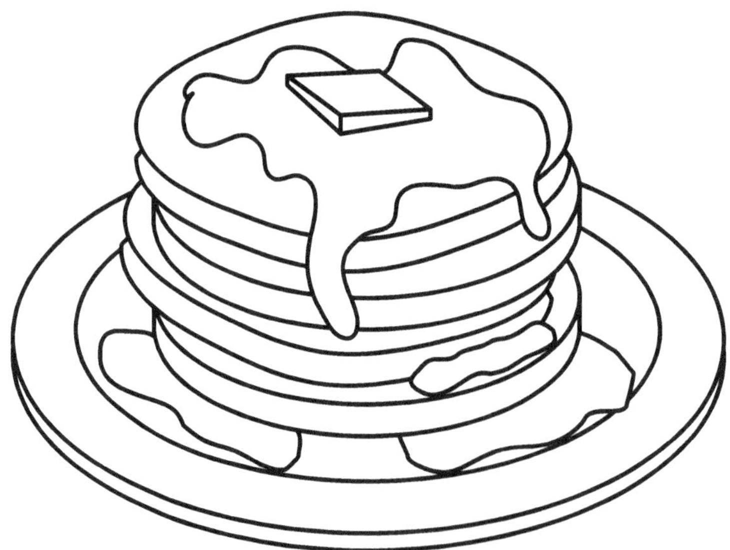

My sight word:

has

 **Read the following sentence!**

She has flowers in her hand.
• • • • • • •

 **Trace and write the sentence!**

She has flowers in her hand.

 **Color the picture!**

My sight word: her

Read the following sentence!

Her sister goes to the doctor.

Trace and write the sentence!

Her sister goes to the doctor.

Color the picture!

My sight word: him

 **Read the following sentence!**

I love him.

 **Trace and write the sentence!**

I love him.

 **Color the picture!**

My sight word: his

Read the following sentence!

The boy eats his lunch.

Trace and write the sentence!

The boy eats his lunch.

Color the picture!

My sight word: **may**

 **Read the following sentence!**

May I borrow your pen?

 **Trace and write the sentence!**

May I borrow your pen?

 **Color the picture!**

My sight word: new

 **Read the following sentence!**

I like your new bike.

 **Trace and write the sentence!**

I like your new bike.

 **Color the picture!**

My sight word: not

Read the following sentence!

You may not go to the beach.

Trace and write the sentence!

You may not go to the beach.

Color the picture!

My sight word: now

Read the following sentence!

Can we talk now?

Trace and write the sentence!

Can we talk now?

Color the picture!

My sight word: old

 **Read the following sentence!**

We should respect old people.

 **Trace and write the sentence!**

We should respect old people.

 **Color the picture!**

My sight word:

one

Read the following sentence!

The baby is one year old.

Trace and write the sentence!

The baby is one year old.

Color the picture!

My sight word: our

Read the following sentence!

Our family is on vacation.

Trace and write the sentence!

Our family is on vacation.

Color the picture!

My sight word:

put

Read the following sentence!

I put the plates on the table.

Trace and write the sentence!

I put the plates on the table.

Color the picture!

My sight word:

red

Read the following sentence!

I like red roses.

Trace and write the sentence!

I like red roses.

Color the picture!

My sight word: run

Read the following sentence!

I run every day because is healthy.

Trace and write the sentence!

I run every day because is healthy.

Color the picture!

My sight word: say

Read the following sentence!

Say hello to your friends.

Trace and write the sentence!

Say hello to your friends.

Color the picture!

My sight word: **see**

Read the following sentence!

I see the school bus.
• • • • •

Trace and write the sentence!

I see the school bus.

Color the picture!

My sight word: she

Read the following sentence!

She is nice and friendly.

Trace and write the sentence!

She is nice and friendly.

Color the picture!

My sight word: sit

Read the following sentence!

May I sit down?
• • • •

Trace and write the sentence!

May I sit down?

Color the picture!

My sight word: six

Read the following sentence!

They have a turtle and six cats.

Trace and write the sentence!

They have a turtle and six cats.

Color the picture!

My sight word: sun

Read the following sentence!

The sun gives us light.

Trace and write the sentence!

The sun gives us light.

Color the picture!

My sight word: ten

Read the following sentence!

This hat costs ten dollars.

Trace and write the sentence!

This hat costs ten dollars.

Color the picture!

My sight word:

the

Read the following sentence!

The plant has beautiful flowers.

Trace and write the sentence!

The plant has beautiful flowers.

Color the picture!

My sight word: too

Read the following sentence!

I eat ice cream too.

Trace and write the sentence!

I eat ice cream too.

Color the picture!

My sight word: try

Read the following sentence!

Try to eat plenty of fresh fruit.

Trace and write the sentence!

Try to eat plenty of fresh fruit.

Color the picture!

My sight word: two

Read the following sentence!

He has two backpacks.

Trace and write the sentence!

He has two backpacks.

Color the picture!

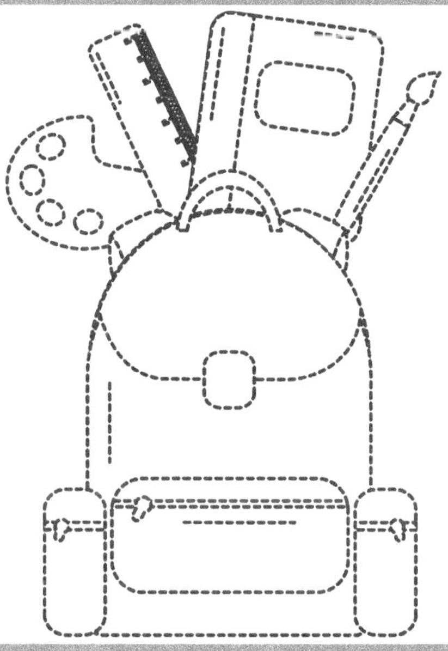

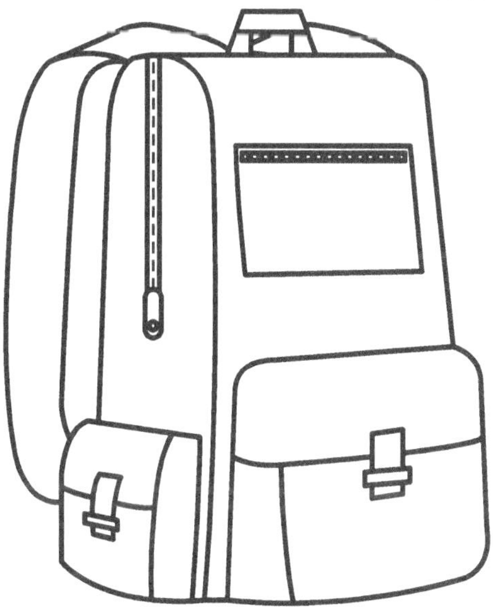

My sight word: use

Read the following sentence!

Can I use your pencil?
• • • • •

Trace and write the sentence!

Can I use your pencil?

Color the picture!

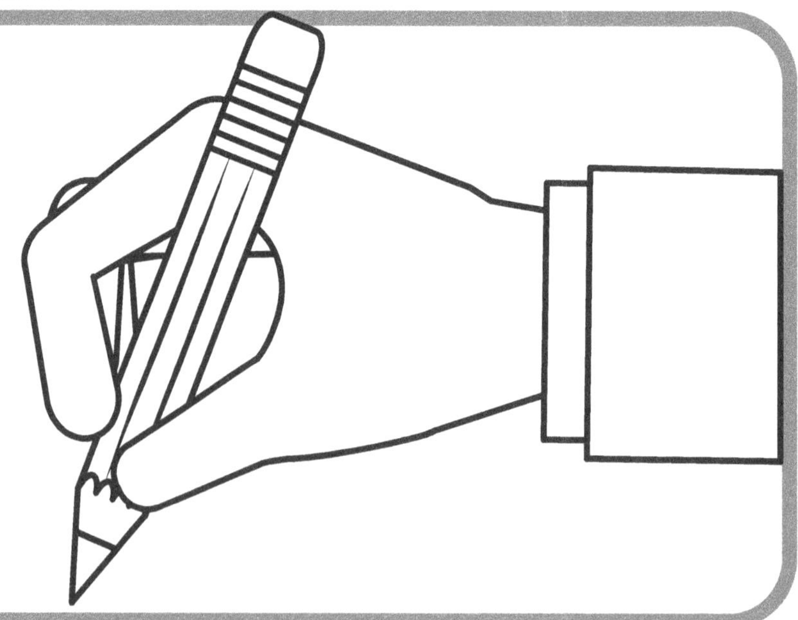

My sight word: was

Read the following sentence!

Maria was listening to a song.

Trace and write the sentence!

Maria was listening to a song.

Color the picture!

My sight word: who

 **Read the following sentence!**

Who closed the door?

 **Trace and write the sentence!**

Who closed the door?

 **Color the picture!**

My sight word: ___ why

Read the following sentence!

Why do you like surfing?

Trace and write the sentence!

Why do you like surfing?

Color the picture!

My sight word: **yes**

Read the following sentence!

We want Tom to say yes.

Trace and write the sentence!

We want Tom to say yes.

Color the picture!

My sight word: you

Read the following sentence!

Thank you for the gifts.

Trace and write the sentence!

Thank you for the gifts.

Color the picture!

Part 4
Write 4 letter words

My sight word:

also

Read the following sentence!

I also love to cook.

Trace and write the sentence!

I also love to cook.

Color the picture!

My sight word: back

Read the following sentence!

I will be back at ten.

Trace and write the sentence!

I will be back at ten.

Color the picture!

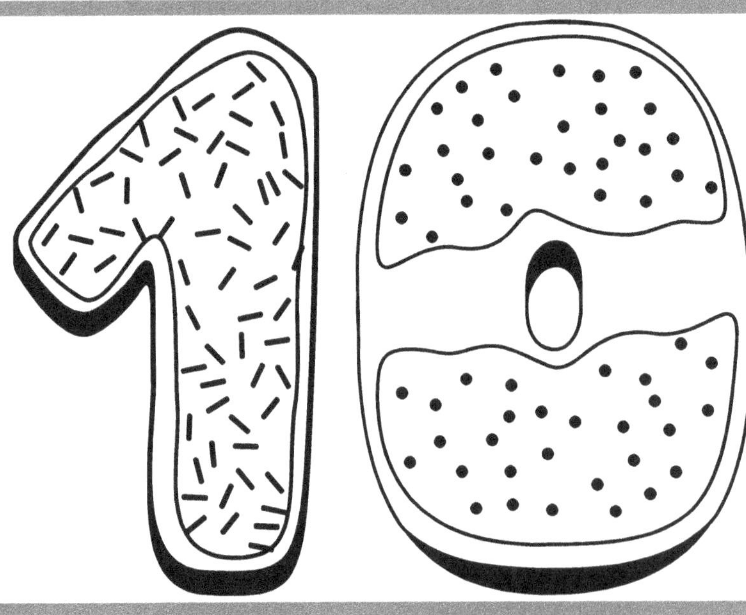

My sight word:

Read the following sentence!

We are best friends.

Trace and write the sentence!

We are best friends.

Color the picture!

My sight word: **book**

Read the following sentence!

The book has a hard cover.
• • • • • •

Trace and write the sentence!

The book has a hard cover.

Color the picture!

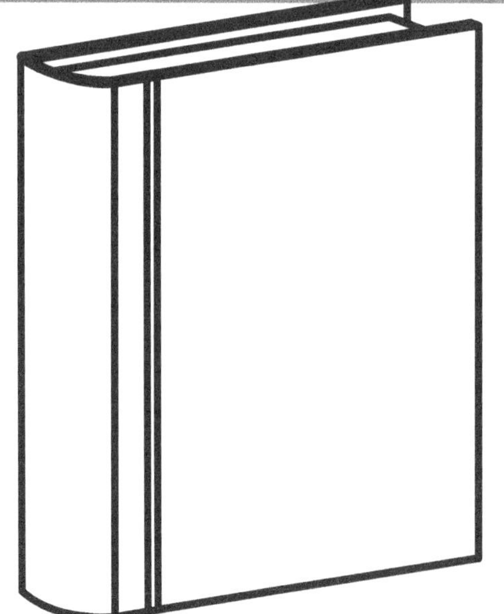

My sight word: both

Read the following sentence!

We are both happy.

Trace and write the sentence!

We are both happy.

Color the picture!

My sight word:

come

Read the following sentence!

I come home from the theatre.

Trace and write the sentence!

I come home from the theatre.

Color the picture!

My sight word: down

Read the following sentence!

He goes down the slide.

Trace and write the sentence!

He goes down the slide.

Color the picture!

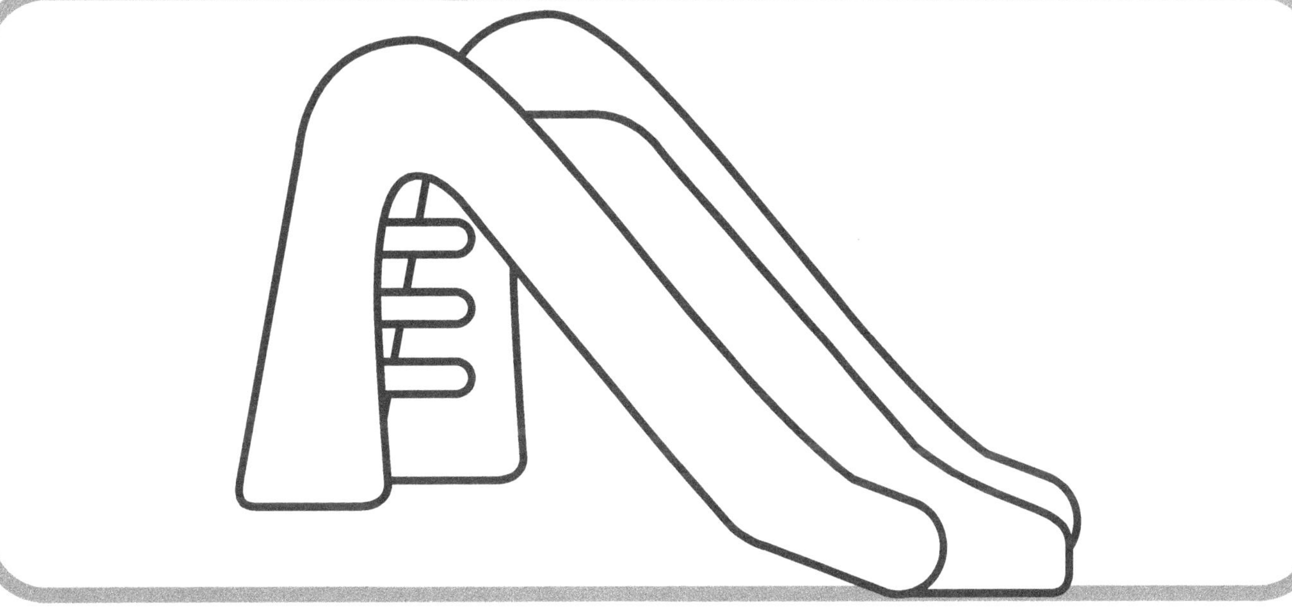

My sight word: each

Read the following sentence!

Each student has a locker.

Trace and write the sentence!

Each student has a locker.

Color the picture!

My sight word: find

Read the following sentence!

I can't find my keys.

Trace and write the sentence!

I can't find my keys.

Color the picture!

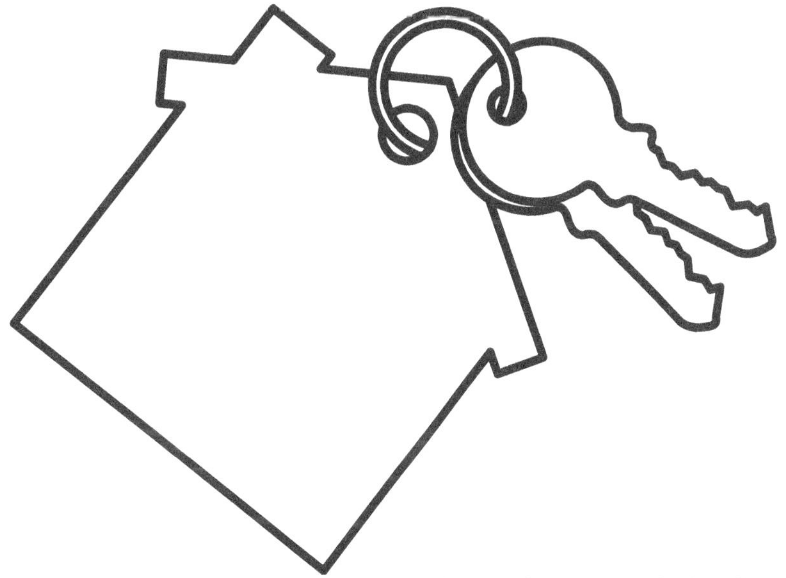

My sight word: **five**

Read the following sentence!

Mike has five crayons.

Trace and write the sentence!

Mike has five crayons.

Color the picture!

My sight word: four

Read the following sentence!

A cow has four legs.

Trace and write the sentence!

A cow has four legs.

Color the picture!

My sight word: **from**

Read the following sentence!

She comes from Europe.

Trace and write the sentence!

She comes from Europe.

Color the picture!

My sight word: give

Read the following sentence!

I will give you my camera.

Trace and write the sentence!

I will give you my camera.

Color the picture!

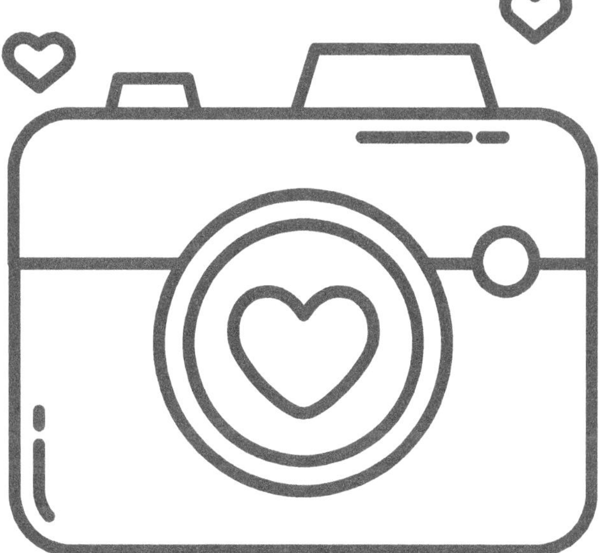

My sight word: good

Read the following sentence!

I am good at reading.

Trace and write the sentence!

I am good at reading.

Color the picture!

My sight word: have

Read the following sentence!

> They have a piano.

Trace and write the sentence!

They have a piano.

Color the picture!

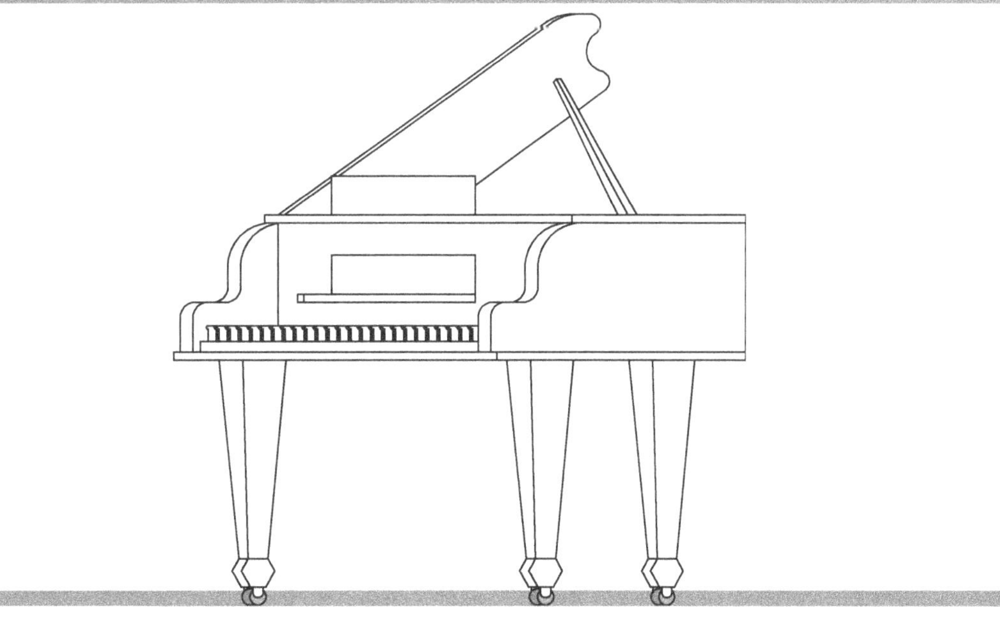

My sight word: help

 **Read the following sentence!**

We help mom with chores.

 **Trace and write the sentence!**

We help mom with chores.

 **Color the picture!**

My sight word: here

 **Read the following sentence!**

Here is a bakery.

 **Trace and write the sentence!**

Here is a bakery.

 **Color the picture!**

My sight word: jump

Read the following sentence!

How high can you jump?

Trace and write the sentence!

How high can you jump?

Color the picture!

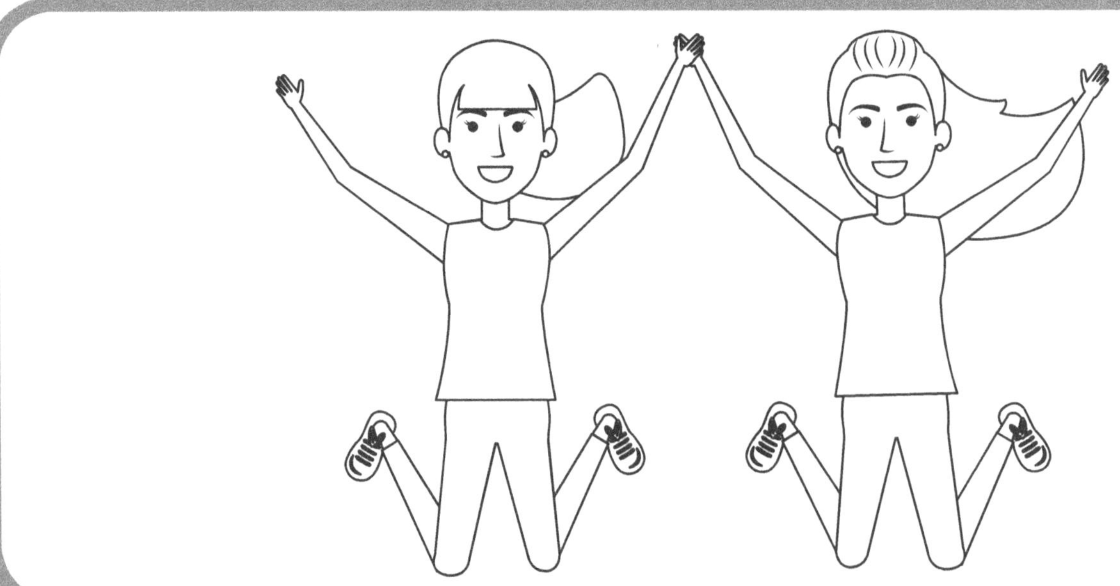

My sight word: **just**

Read the following sentence!

I am just watching TV.

Trace and write the sentence!

I am just watching TV.

Color the picture!

My sight word: keep

Read the following sentence!

You must keep your room tidy.

Trace and write the sentence!

You must keep your room tidy.

Color the picture!

My sight word: know

 **Read the following sentence!**

I know all the letters.

 **Trace and write the sentence!**

I know all the letters

 **Color the picture!**

My sight word: like

Read the following sentence!

I like baby goats.

Trace and write the sentence!

I like baby goats.

Color the picture!

My sight word: live

 **Read the following sentence!**

We live on a farm.

 **Trace and write the sentence!**

We live on a farm.

 **Color the picture!**

My sight word:

look

Read the following sentence!

Look at my watch.

Trace and write the sentence!

Look at my watch.

Color the picture!

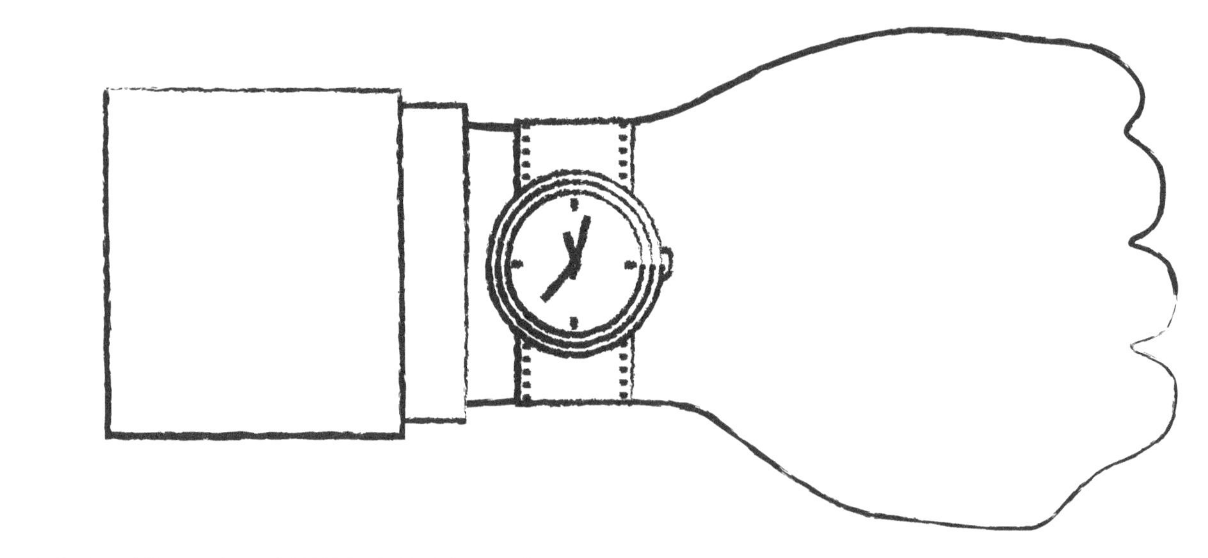

My sight word:

make

Read the following sentence!

We make peanut butter cookies.

Trace and write the sentence!

We make peanut butter cookies.

Color the picture!

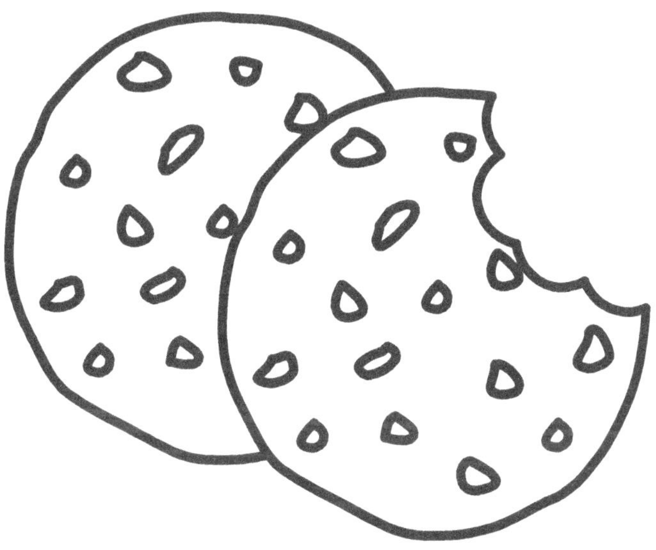

My sight word: many

Read the following sentence!

How many kids do you have?

Trace and write the sentence!

How many kids do you have?

Color the picture!

My sight word: much

Read the following sentence!

I like tennis very much.

Trace and write the sentence!

I like tennis very much.

Color the picture!

My sight word: must

Read the following sentence!

We must fasten our seatbelts.

Trace and write the sentence!

We must fasten our seatbelts.

Color the picture!

My sight word: nine

Read the following sentence!

He has nine shirts.

Trace and write the sentence!

He has nine shirts.

Color the picture!

My sight word: read

Read the following sentence!

You can read and write.

Trace and write the sentence!

You can read and write.

Color the picture!

My sight word: show

 **Read the following sentence!**

Can you show me your drawings?

 **Trace and write the sentence!**

Can you show me your drawings?

 **Color the picture!**

My sight word:

sing

Read the following sentence!

She likes to sing old songs.
• • • • • •

Trace and write the sentence!

She likes to sing old songs.

Color the picture!

My sight word: soon

Read the following sentence!

I will see my parents soon.

Trace and write the sentence!

I will see my parents soon.

Color the picture!

My sight word: stop

 **Read the following sentence!**

This is a stop sign.

 **Trace and write the sentence!**

This is a stop sign.

 **Color the picture!**

My sight word: **such**

Read the following sentence!

The baby has such beautiful toys.

Trace and write the sentence!

The baby has such beautiful toys.

Color the picture!

My sight word: take

Read the following sentence!

Let's take a trip to the zoo.

Trace and write the sentence!

Let's take a trip to the zoo.

Color the picture!

My sight word: tell

Read the following sentence!

Please tell me a new story.

Trace and write the sentence!

Please tell me a new story.

Color the picture!

My sight word: than

Read the following sentence!

My brother is taller than me.
•   •   •   •   •   •

Trace and write the sentence!

My brother is taller than me.

Color the picture!

My sight word: that

Read the following sentence!

That is a beautiful tree.

Trace and write the sentence!

That is a beautiful tree.

Color the picture!

My sight word: them

 **Read the following sentence!**

I will help them with karate lessons.

 **Trace and write the sentence!**

I will help them with karate lessons.

 **Color the picture!**

My sight word: they

Read the following sentence!

They clean the garden together.

Trace and write the sentence!

They clean the garden together.

Color the picture!

My sight word: very

Read the following sentence!

It is very cold outside.

Trace and write the sentence!

It is very cold outside.

Color the picture!

My sight word: want

Read the following sentence!

I want a guitar.

Trace and write the sentence!

I want a guitar.

Color the picture!

My sight word:

wash

Read the following sentence!

Dad and I wash the car.

Trace and write the sentence!

Dad and I wash the car.

Color the picture!

My sight word: **were**

Read the following sentence!

You were playing with your friends.

Trace and write the sentence!

You were playing with your friends.

Color the picture!

My sight word: **will**

Read the following sentence!

I will be home for dinner.

Trace and write the sentence!

I will be home for dinner.

Color the picture!

My sight word:

wish

 **Read the following sentence!**

Make a wish.

 **Trace and write the sentence!**

Make a wish.

 **Color the picture!**

My sight word: **with**

Read the following sentence!

She goes to the airport with him.

Trace and write the sentence!

She goes to the airport with him.

Color the picture!

My sight word: work

Read the following sentence!

My aunt works at the pharmacy.

Trace and write the sentence!

My aunt works at the pharmacy.

Color the picture!

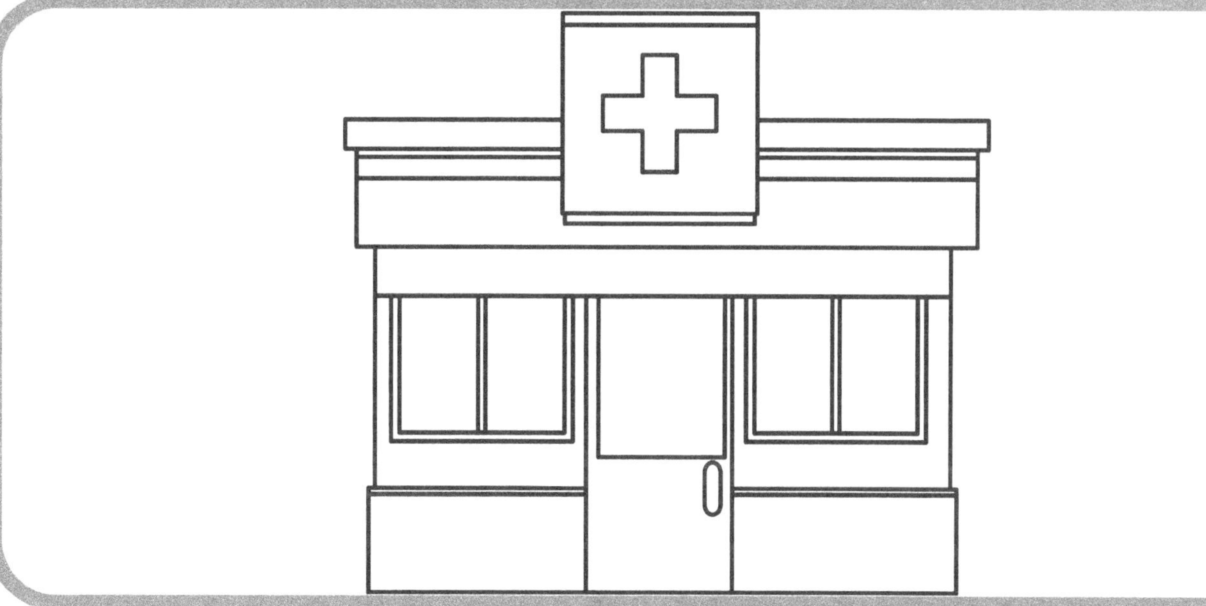

My sight word: your

Read the following sentence!

Is this your doll?
• • • •

Trace and write the sentence!

Is this your doll?

Color the picture!

Part 5
Write 5 & 6 letter words

My sight word: about

Read the following sentence!

I want to talk about baseball.

Trace and write the sentence!

I want to talk about baseball.

Color the picture!

My sight word: above

Read the following sentence!

The plane flies above the clouds.

Trace and write the sentence!

The plane flies above the clouds.

Color the picture!

My sight word: after

Read the following sentence!

I will eat dessert after dinner.

Trace and write the sentence!

I will eat dessert after dinner.

Color the picture!

My sight word: again

 **Read the following sentence!**

It's raining again.

 **Trace and write the sentence!**

It's raining again.

 **Color the picture!**

My sight word: almost

 **Read the following sentence!**

Almost everyone has a computer.

 **Trace and write the sentence!**

Almost everyone has a computer.

 **Color the picture!**

My sight word: along

Read the following sentence!

The ship sails along the coast.

Trace and write the sentence!

The ship sails along the coast.

Color the picture!

My sight word:

always

Read the following sentence!

He is always on time.

Trace and write the sentence!

He is always on time.

Color the picture!

My sight word: answer

Read the following sentence!

I answer correctly in class.
• • • • •

Trace and write the sentence!

I answer correctly in class.

Color the picture!

My sight word: around

Read the following sentence!

He drives around the city.

Trace and write the sentence!

He drives around the city.

Color the picture!

My sight word: become

Read the following sentence!

I will become a nurse.

Trace and write the sentence!

I will become a nurse.

Color the picture!

My sight word:

before

Read the following sentence!

Call me before you leave.

Trace and write the sentence!

Call me before you leave.

Color the picture!

My sight word:

begin

Read the following sentence!

The play will begin soon.

Trace and write the sentence!

The play will begin soon.

Color the picture!

My sight word: better

Read the following sentence!

He swims better than I do.

Trace and write the sentence!

He swims better than I do.

Color the picture!

My sight word: black

 **Read the following sentence!**

His shoes are black.

 **Trace and write the sentence!**

His shoes are black.

 **Color the picture!**

My sight word: bring

Read the following sentence!

I bring lunch to school.

Trace and write the sentence!

I bring lunch to school.

Color the picture!

My sight word: brown

Read the following sentence!

The bear is brown.

Trace and write the sentence!

The bear is brown.

Color the picture!

My sight word: carry

Read the following sentence!

I carry my bag.

Trace and write the sentence!

I carry my bag.

Color the picture!

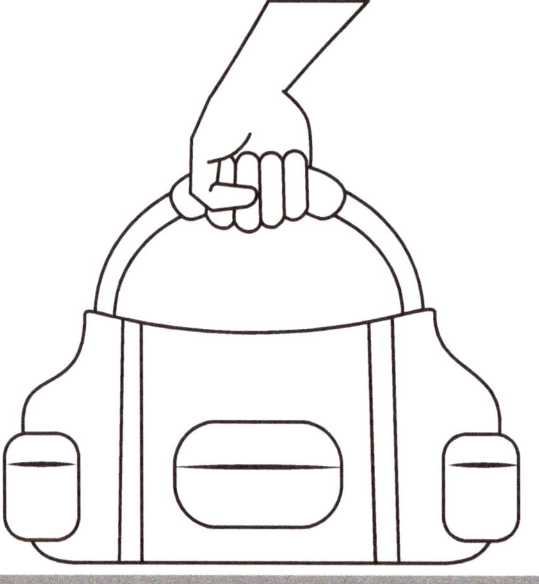

My sight word: change

Read the following sentence!

We change our clothes.

Trace and write the sentence!

We change our clothes.

Color the picture!

My sight word: clean

Read the following sentence!

The kids clean their room.

Trace and write the sentence!

The kids clean their room.

Color the picture!

My sight word: close

Read the following sentence!

I close the door.

Trace and write the sentence!

I close the door.

Color the picture!

My sight word: drink

Read the following sentence!

They drink coffee.

Trace and write the sentence!

They drink coffee.

Color the picture!

My sight word: early

Read the following sentence!

I get up early.

Trace and write the sentence!

I get up early.

Color the picture!

My sight word: earth

Read the following sentence!

The earth is round.

Trace and write the sentence!

The earth is round.

Color the picture!

My sight word: eight

Read the following sentence!

An octopus has eight tentacles.

Trace and write the sentence!

An octopus has eight tentacles.

Color the picture!

My sight word: every

 **Read the following sentence!**

I eat fruit every day.

 **Trace and write the sentence!**

I eat fruit every day.

 **Color the picture!**

My sight word: first

Read the following sentence!

I have won first prize.

Trace and write the sentence!

I have won first prize.

Color the picture!

My sight word: follow

Read the following sentence!

The dog follows her.

Trace and write the sentence!

The dog follows her.

Color the picture!

My sight word: front

Read the following sentence!

The front door is open.

Trace and write the sentence!

The front door is open.

Color the picture!

My sight word: funny

Read the following sentence!

Tom is really funny.

Trace and write the sentence!

Tom is really funny.

Color the picture!

My sight word:

Read the following sentence!

You do a great job.

Trace and write the sentence!

You do a great job.

Color the picture!

My sight word: house

Read the following sentence!

Her house is beautiful.

Trace and write the sentence!

Her house is beautiful.

Color the picture!

My sight word: large

Read the following sentence!

This plant grows large.

Trace and write the sentence!

This plant grows large.

Color the picture!

My sight word: laugh

Read the following sentence!

We laugh at your jokes.
· · · · ·

Trace and write the sentence!

We laugh at your jokes.

Color the picture!

My sight word: learn

Read the following sentence!

I learn to write sentences.

Trace and write the sentence!

I learn to write sentences.

Color the picture!

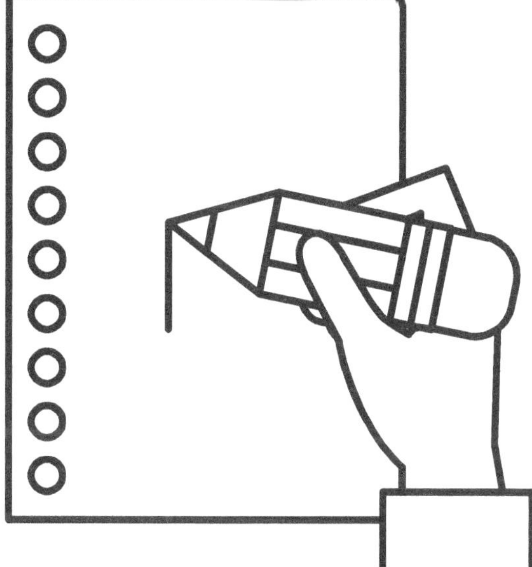

My sight word: leave

Read the following sentence!

You can leave the window open.

Trace and write the sentence!

You can leave the window open.

Color the picture!

My sight word: light

Read the following sentence!

The sun gives us light.
· · · · ·

Trace and write the sentence!

The sun gives us light.

Color the picture!

My sight word:

Read the following sentence!

We are little children.

Trace and write the sentence!

We are little children.

Color the picture!

My sight word: never

Read the following sentence!

I never eat my broccoli.

Trace and write the sentence!

I never eat my broccoli.

Color the picture!

My sight word: night

Read the following sentence!

It is a cold night.

Trace and write the sentence!

It is a cold night.

Color the picture!

My sight word: number

Read the following sentence!

Mike knows my number.

Trace and write the sentence!

Mike knows my number.

Color the picture!

My sight word: often

Read the following sentence!

I often read books.

Trace and write the sentence!

I often read books.

Color the picture!

My sight word: paper

Read the following sentence!

I use paper bags.

Trace and write the sentence!

I use paper bags.

Color the picture!

My sight word: people

Read the following sentence!

Be kind to old people.

Trace and write the sentence!

Be kind to old people.

Color the picture!

My sight word: plant

Read the following sentence!

This plant is good to eat.

Trace and write the sentence!

This plant is good to eat.

Color the picture!

My sight word: please

Read the following sentence!

A cup of tea, please.
•   •   •   •   •

Trace and write the sentence!

A cup of tea, please.

Color the picture!

My sight word: **pretty**

Read the following sentence!

Mary is a pretty girl.

Trace and write the sentence!

Mary is a pretty girl.

Color the picture!

My sight word: right

Read the following sentence!

My right hand hurts.

Trace and write the sentence!

My right hand hurts.

Color the picture!

My sight word: river

Read the following sentence!

Tom went down the river in a canoe.

Trace and write the sentence!

Tom went down the river in a canoe.

Color the picture!

My sight word: round

Read the following sentence!

We bought a round table.

Trace and write the sentence!

We bought a round table.

Color the picture!

My sight word: seven

Read the following sentence!

There are seven continents.

Trace and write the sentence!

There are seven continents.

Color the picture!

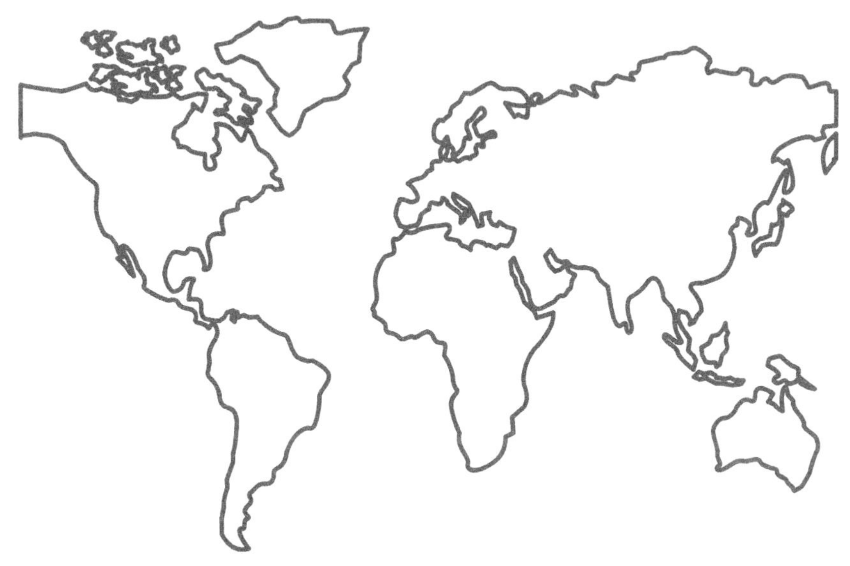

My sight word: sleep

Read the following sentence!

I had a good sleep.

Trace and write the sentence!

There are seven continents.

Color the picture!

My sight word: small

Read the following sentence!

Her hands are small.

Trace and write the sentence!

Her hands are small.

Color the picture!

My sight word: sound

Read the following sentence!

Tom sounds funny.

Trace and write the sentence!

Tom sounds funny.

Color the picture!

My sight word: spell

Read the following sentence!

Please spell your name.
•   •   •   •

Trace and write the sentence!

Please spell your name.

Color the picture!

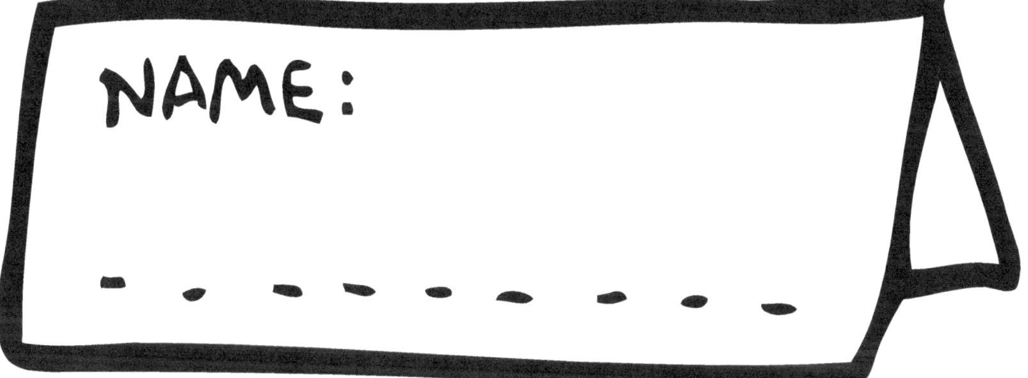

My sight word: start

Read the following sentence!

Let's start running .

Trace and write the sentence!

Let's start running .

Color the picture!

My sight word:

still

Read the following sentence!

The cat is still hungry.

Trace and write the sentence!

The cat is still hungry.

Color the picture!

My sight word: story

Read the following sentence!

I like your story.
• • • •

Trace and write the sentence!

I like your story.

Color the picture!

My sight word: street

Read the following sentence!

They live on my street.

Trace and write the sentence!

They live on my street.

Color the picture!

My sight word: thank

 **Read the following sentence!**

Thank you for this gift.

 **Trace and write the sentence!**

Thank you for this gift.

 **Color the picture!**

My sight word: there

 **Read the following sentence!**

I want to go there.

 **Trace and write the sentence!**

I want to go there.

 **Color the picture!**

My sight word: these

 **Read the following sentence!**

These socks do not match.

 **Trace and write the sentence!**

These socks do not match.

 **Color the picture!**

My sight word: think

Read the following sentence!

I think I'm sick.

Trace and write the sentence!

I think I'm sick.

Color the picture!

My sight word: those

Read the following sentence!

Those shoes are grey.

Trace and write the sentence!

Those shoes are grey.

Color the picture!

My sight word: three

Read the following sentence!

Our neighbor has three sons.

Trace and write the sentence!

Our neighbor has three sons.

Color the picture!

My sight word: today

Read the following sentence!

We will meet today.

Trace and write the sentence!

We will meet today.

Color the picture!

My sight word: under

Read the following sentence!

The cat is under the chair.

Trace and write the sentence!

The cat is under the chair.

Color the picture!

My sight word: until

Read the following sentence!

I thought you'd sleep until noon.

Trace and write the sentence!

I thought youd sleep until noon.

Color the picture!

My sight word: watch

Read the following sentence!

Tom has a pocket watch.

Trace and write the sentence!

Tom has a pocket watch.

Color the picture!

My sight word: where

Read the following sentence!

Where is my phone?

Trace and write the sentence!

Where is my phone?

Color the picture!

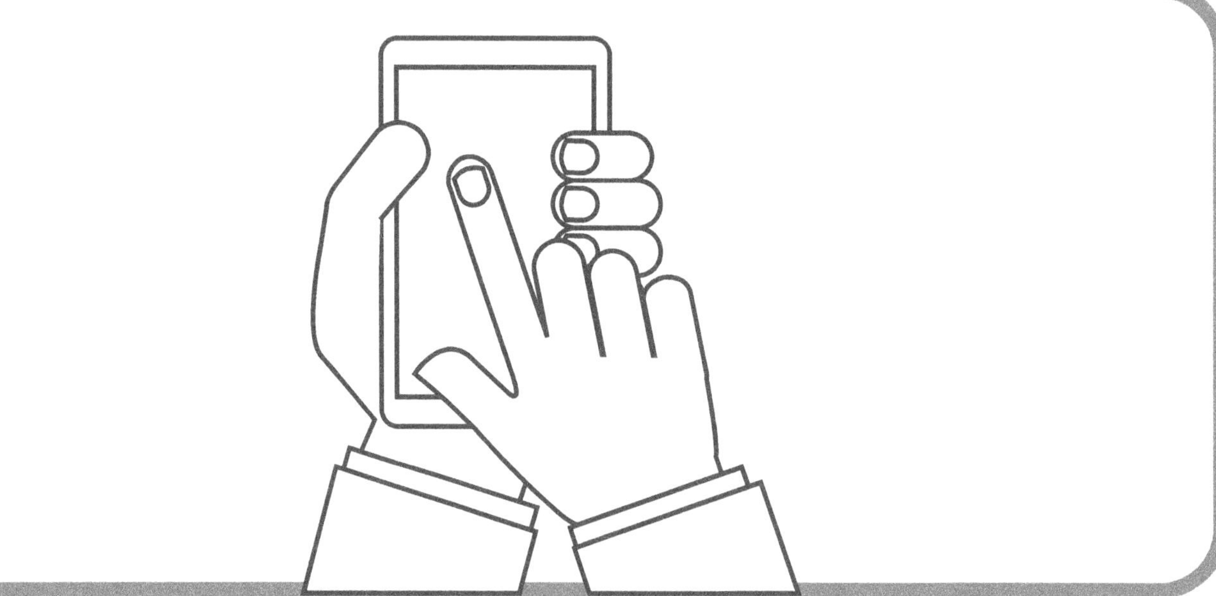

My sight word: which

Read the following sentence!

Which is your guitar?

Trace and write the sentence!

Which is your guitar?

Color the picture!

My sight word: while

Read the following sentence!

Do not read while walking

Trace and write the sentence!

Do not read while walking

Color the picture!

My sight word: white

Read the following sentence!

Her hair is white.

Trace and write the sentence!

Her hair is white.

Color the picture!

My sight word: write

Read the following sentence!

I could write a book.

Trace and write the sentence!

I could write a book.

Color the picture!

Congratulation on completing this workbook!

Don't forget to claim one of our free, ready-to-print certificates and reward your child's effort in completing our workbook. Access the link below or scan the QR code to get your free bonus!

https://mailchi.mp/12abf0326fc4/certificate-of-completion